What Others Are Saying About *God's Got It*

Wow, what a remarkable and touching journey! Reginald Simmons was an amazing example of what life is truly about. Now I better understand the impact he made on his daughter, Sheri Powell, my friend and author of this book. He certainly paid it forward in his endeavors to help and encourage others. Once I started reading, I couldn't stop. I just wanted to know what was going to happen on his next adventure. So grateful that even though I didn't know him, he left his footprint in the sand. His legacy goes on as his ways of loving, caring, and praying for others has been passed down to the next generation. Sheri, thank you for the times we've had doughnuts and coffee, and talked about life and the Lord. It definitely has new meaning from this point on.

—Kimberly Mathews,
Life Coach

Another standing ovation, my sister!

Riveting – a story of unconditional love. Forgiveness by God's grace and mercy between a dad and his princess for things seen and unseen. Blessed to have known Mr. Simmons; a wise man with a kind and gentle spirit. What a blessing that he journaled, leaving his family with such a legacy of his innermost thoughts and prayers in the midst of trials, tribulations, health issues, and a mental illness which he didn't allow to obscure him from loving & trusting the Lord. Sheri, such an inspiring story for all! Kudos for the information and links on mental health to help others. Education is an invaluable key!

—Sharon Tyson,
Executive Assistant

GOD'S GOT IT!

DON'T WORRY ABOUT ANYTHING

Additional books by Sheri Powell

Pausing With God: A Journey Through Menopause (English)

Pausing With God: A Journey Through Menopause (Spanish)

Pausing In His Presence: A Shut-In Experience

A Woman of Excellence: The Ministry of My Mother

God's Got It

Don't Worry About Anything

Sheri Powell

Published by
SLP Company, Fleming Island, Florida

God's Got It: Don't Worry About Anything
Copyright 2020 Sheri Powell

Cover design: Christine Dupre (www.vidagraphicdesign.com)
Editor: Barbara Hollace (www.barbarahollace.com)
Interior design: Russel Davis (Gray Dog Press, www.graydogpress.com)
Photographer (author photo): William McCoy (Combatcasual@gmail.com)
Printer: Ingram Spark

ISBN: 978-0-578-88568-1 (Paperback)
ISBN: 978-0-578-92634-6 (eBook)
Library of Congress Control Number: 2021906766

For more information or to contact the author:
Email: PausingWithGod@gmail.com
Or by mail: Pausing With God Ministries, Inc.
C/O Sheri Powell
P. O. Box 9172
Fleming Island, FL 32006

When you PAUSE, visit our website: www.PausingWithGod.com

Printed in the United States of America
First Printing 05/2021

Dedication

This book is dedicated to you – Dad. Though we had our ups and downs, your love kept pouring into my empty, and sometimes, half-filled cup. I am blessed that I get to share your prayers and thoughts with our readers.

Thomas Fuller is quoted as saying, "If you have one true friend, you have more than your share." Over the years friendship has been compartmentalized as acquaintance, colleague, and true friend. A true friend is commonly known as somebody you can depend on in the good, the bad, and ugly seasons of your life. Someone who despite the differences you may have, always has your best interest at heart.

For years, I learned a lot about the meaning of a true friend from you, Dad. Though you and Mom divorced when I was a little girl, it was our weekends and holiday visits that permitted me to observe and admire how you were so intentional and deliberate about how you treated people.

You had very few enemies, because you believed it was worth having a conversation with anyone who was in your midst for any period of time.

One of the qualities that those who knew you would say, is that you accepted people for who they were, not for who others thought they should be. You didn't allow their struggles or trials to dictate or hinder you from getting to know them, but rather their current situation presented you with an opportunity to invite them to join you at your favorite coffee shop.

People found that your company was as warm as the cup of coffee in their hands and conversations with you were stirred with wisdom and so sweet to the ear.

Dad, I know it was your prayer as well as mine, that those who hold this book in their hands will do more than just turn the pages.

Thank you, Dad, for trusting me enough to share what is necessary and the discernment to keep in my heart your thoughts that are only meant for me to behold. I am truly rich as you have left me with this priceless gift that is a blessing to me and for generations yet to come.

May these words leap into your heart (especially the heart of fathers) and motivate you to take time to have a cup of your favorite beverage with someone (perhaps your daughter) and make "journal worthy" kind of memories.

~Sheri Powell

Foreword

Make yourself a cup of coffee or grab your favorite beverage and take a seat. Though it would take me an eternity to share all about my brother, I'm going to attempt to give you the Reader's Digest version.

Reggie's motto was that there was no better way to start out your day than by sharing a cup of coffee accompanied by a glazed donut with someone you love dearly.

My brother used these two delicacies as a catalyst to fellowship with family and friends.

I remember the smile those times of fellowship would bring to our mother's face. Every day, after work at the same time, you saw her shuffling around with anticipation as she awaited his arrival. After work, my brother would come over with his bag of goodies, but what our mother really looked forward to was their fellowship.

How could something so small but so intentional bring such great pleasure? Their conversations were like none other. Always filled with laughter, serious exchanges, or dialogues, but would always end how they started, about God.

One of the many things our mom did was to pass along her love for God to all of her children. Reggie soaked it up like a sponge. You would find him regularly reading God's Word (the Bible).

Reggie was like most kids who wanted to grow up before their time. I can remember two incidents that we both laughed about for years.

Incident #1: All of our siblings had moved out and my brother and I were the last ones living at home. Reggie considered himself the man of the house (our protector). This particular evening, he got up to go to the restroom and I realized that I had to go also. I crawled out of my bed, still drowsy. As I walked toward the bathroom, I realized someone was in there . . . it was him, my baby brother. I stood by the door and waited patiently for him to come out.

Mr. Protector opened the door, and out of nowhere, he hollered so loud that he scared me. Reggie later said, he was so frightened because he thought someone had broken into the house. Moral of this story: My brother realized that growing up came with unexpected surprises, especially behind closed doors.

Incident #2: I used to work at Joe's BBQ from 6 p.m. till midnight. My job was located across from a jazz club called the Monterey. My brother Reggie loved music. One night after I got off work, guess who was standing outside, dressed to the nines (a saying back in the day). Though Reggie was too young to get into the club, he didn't let that keep him from enjoying the sounds coming from inside. There he stood outdoors, tapping his feet to the beat of the music.

Still too young to be the man of the house or the protector that he thought he should be, Reggie was faithful in holding down a job to help provide income for our home, this sacrifice didn't go unnoticed. Over the years, my brother had his trials and tribulations, but he never wavered from knowing that God was going to take care of him. I can still hear him say, "Babe, I don't want for nothing, God's Got It!"

—Betty M. Ford (Auntie Babe, Dad's fourth sister)

Contents

C-O-F-F-E-E

Did you know you have a few good reasons to drink coffee, within moderation. Coffee is known to increase one's mental function, energy level, and mood.

You may be shocked to find out that coffee contains many nutrients: B2, B5, manganese, potassium, and niacin. It is also said to help lower blood sugar levels and offer protection from Alzheimer's disease and dementia.

One of the things I didn't know is that coffee is the biggest source of antioxidants. Want to know why they are important? Antioxidants are substances that may protect your cells against free radicals, which may play a role in heart disease, cancer, and other diseases. Free radicals are molecules produced when your body breaks down food or when you're exposed to tobacco smoke or radiation.

Not sure what time of day you prefer to consume your cup. I like mine in the morning, but I have been known to drink this tasty beverage any time throughout the day. Instead of a night cap or glass of warm milk, I can drink a freshly brewed cup of java at bedtime and still fall fast asleep.

Humor me, and let's take a look and see the slight resemblance of the life of a coffee bean to that of homo sapiens. It takes some time for us human beings from birth to develop and grow into who we were created to be.

For the coffee bean, there is a process from seed to cup. There's the planting, harvesting, processing, drying, milling, exporting, tasting, roasting, grinding, and finally, the brewing.

We can find ourselves being subjected to some of the same processes as the coffee bean. Starting with a tiny seed, we are held in a nursery until we are delivered to our place of tenancy. When planted in the right nutrients, it is then we are able to grow.

Over the years, our harvesting process can be experienced in one of two ways: strip or selective picking. Strip picking is exactly how it sounds. Our situations, trials, and circumstances have a way of revealing a great many areas of our lives: the good, the bad, and the ugly. Areas wherein we may need a little more time to mature or flourish.

There is also selective picking. This involves the persnickety areas in our lives. Within the picking, additional steps follow: the processing, drying, and milling out. This is where what we try to conceal is revealed. Though it can be emotionally and mentally taxing, as we make the necessary adjustments in the midst of each challenge and their unsolicited consequences, the outcome often has a positive impact. It is here that we find that our perception, understanding, and responses have changed. We are learning how to tear down the barriers that keep us from living simply, so we can simply live.

Once we are settled in a comfortable place knowing who we are, we find the shell of the old man is falling away and the new man is breaking through. During this process, others begin to notice that a change is taking place. It's a season where we don't mind sharing our transformation in hopes that it will encourage them. What we have learned in the process (life-lessons) can be referred to as the tasting stage. As we become used to taking refuge in the Lord, sipping on the cup He has for us (which is for our good and for His glory), we discover that He is always good and can be depended upon no matter what stage of life we find ourselves.

Though life can leave a bitter taste in one's mouth, each season is an opportunity for us to get to know God and draw us closer to His plans and purposes for our lives. Although sometimes we would like to, there isn't any way to circumvent the process of growing into all we were created to be. As long as we have breath in our lungs, we will taste and experience seasons, just like the coffee bean, that involve planting, harvesting, processing, drying, milling, exporting, tasting, roasting, grinding, and finally, the brewing.

But it is in the brewing that others become aware of our scent. They see that each season of our lives has become a concoction that produced growth and maturity. Our perspective changes and our life experiences are viewed as a privilege and less of a responsibility, so that we become and continue to be a sweet-smelling aroma that draws others to taste and see that the Lord is good (Psalm 34:8).

His-Story

Reginald Lionel Simmons was born January 26, 1940 in New Haven, Connecticut. Dad journaled that he had a very enjoyable youth while attending New Haven Public Schools and then graduating from James Hillhouse High School in 1958.

He married my mom in 1961, and several years later, Dad became ill and was forced to stop working for a while. Dad loved to work, and for a number of years, he went back and forth between times of being gainfully employed to suddenly unemployed.

When working or in between jobs, Dad frequented a coffee shop, which became his favorite spot. My dad made it a habit, at a minimum, to greet, if not hold a conversation with each one of the establishment's clientele. Even when money was tight, Dad would offer them a cup of coffee and listen to them share about their lives. Some of their stories were ones of satisfaction, and others, were full of complaints, but Dad always tried to leave them with a word of encouragement.

Some years later, I was sitting in my favorite coffee shop with the coffee aroma swirling around my nose. As I took a sip, a smile came to my face. I was reminded that even on my darkest days, when I didn't know how this or that was going to work out, no matter how small or large the situation appeared, Dad's words encouraged me. I remembered one of Dad's favorite sayings, "Sheri, don't worry about anything, God's Got It." Now looking back, I realize that in spite of many years of difficulties, I thought it, but now, I know it. I know without a hint of doubt that I don't have to worry about anything, "God's Got It."

Dad's journey included seasons of being employed and unemployed, and good health and illness, until one day he fell ill and had to cease from ever working again. For more than thirty years, doctors tried to pinpoint what exactly was going on. Time after time, my dad was misdiagnosed and mistreated. This took a toll on him and those closest to him.

All Dad wanted was some amount of financial stability, so that he could be an asset, and not a hindrance to his family. After much consideration, Dad finally applied for and was granted Social Security benefits. Dad mentioned in his journal how this brought him great comfort as he began to figure out where he fit in this crazy world.

Till Death Did They Part

The pages are tattered and torn. In an effort to prevent them from falling on the floor, with both hands, I held the front and back covers together. With one hand holding the left side and the other the right, I carefully turned the page. On the inside at the top, there in bold-italic letters was a title, "Family." I scanned each line, reading the names and the dates. The first entry was from 1961. I shook my head slowly from side to side, to gain clarity. I was baffled, "Hmmm, I wasn't even born yet." I continued and saw that there was a brief note after each name that could be construed as a prayer. "Dear God, thank you for my family. I thank you for my kids and even my ex-wife. I know things haven't turned out the way they should have, but I'm grateful that I have them in my life."

Our parents had married and divorced when my siblings and I were very young. As I continued reading, it became evident that the law or a piece of paper could not stop people from loving one another. I mention "according to the law" because after all these years, Dad not only kept this Bible in his possession, but he held just as close, the love the two of them shared. This became more evident as Mom's illness progressed.

Even though Dad was not well himself, he was with me almost every day. Dad spent hours with me at the hospital, convalescent, and rehabilitation centers. Dad made sure Mom had what she needed, and at times even what she wanted, even if it was against the doctor's orders. With each visit, you'd see in their countenances that they looked forward to one another's company. You'd never know that they had been divorced for over 30 years. Though there were tumultuous times, that was water under the bridge; they were now speaking of one another as if they were still married.

I didn't understand how vital his company was until one particular day of a hospital stay. Mom's quality of life was not what her attending physicians would have liked it to be. One of the nurses came in the room. She looked around and asked if I could step outside for a moment. Dad followed me.

"The only thing keeping your mom alive is dialysis. If we stop the treatment, she will not live. So, we are suggesting that since we don't anticipate her getting any better or having any good quality of life, our recommendation is to let her go. Stop the dialysis and let things take their course." The nurse communicated this with little to no compassion.

I was numb. I didn't know how to respond. Clearly this nurse didn't understand or consider our beliefs or even my mom's wishes. I get it, the nurse was coming from a medical standpoint. When you deal with these types of situations on a daily basis, it can be void of any bedside manner.

I haven't seen that look in his eyes but a few times. Dad gently grabbed me by the arm and took me down the hallway away from Mom's room. He pulled me to the side. Not knowing what Dad was about to say, I leaned on the wall. "The only person that can take a life is God, and when He is ready for your mom, He will come and get her," he said, in a firm tone of voice.

It wasn't an opinion; it was a command to let nature take its course. We returned to the room and unapologetically communicated to the nurse that the dialysis was to continue, and they were to do whatever was necessary to keep Mom alive.

This incident, and several others, encouraged me that for Mom and Dad, the divorce didn't end their love for one another; it was literally till death did they part!

God's Got It

Life is funny. When you are born, it is your parents who take care of you and carry the concern of what kind of adult you will become. It's not until we are grown and with our own families, that we wake up to the realization that the tables will one day turn. Most adults will have the opportunity to take care of their parents (especially if their health is not good) and often we find ourselves uneasy about how they will live the rest of their lives.

This is my July 2019, 9:27 p.m. journal entry.

"I turned in my FMLA paperwork. There is no reason for
me to doubt that it will be approved. I almost felt guilty
about asking for so much time, but I quickly shook off those
feelings. I cannot afford to miss this opportunity to see about
Dad. He's 79 and only God knows how much longer he has
on this side of the earth. Besides, this is our chance to gather
and make some memories with him and my family."

Dad had an accident and I wanted to be there to do whatever I could. With the distance between us, he in Connecticut and me in Florida, it was hard to detect what frame of mind he was really in. My phone conversations with aides, nurses, and doctors were contradictory and made me cautiously suspicious. All I knew was that I had to get to my dad.

As I prepped for the trip, I made some tentative notes, drafting a plan of action to take once I arrived. I tried to pray and lay my thoughts aside, but my mind raced through each scenario trying to attach a possible solution. What if Dad is in bad shape and can no longer take care of himself? What if he cannot resume living on his own?

A memory of a conversation Dad and I had years ago came to my mind. Dad made me promise that when he got old, that I would never put him in a facility that would strip him of his freedom to come and go as he pleased. What about that promise? Would Dad remember, and if so, would he hold me to it? What if he "this" and what if he "that" . . . rolled through my head until I dozed off to sleep.

Some hours later, my alarm went off. My eyes were closed, but my mind was fully awake. I threw one foot at a time, left then right, out of the bed. I headed for the mirror on the wall. Staring at my reflection, though it all felt like a dream, feelings of worry crept in.

Everything was packed. I filled the car with my luggage and before leaving for the airport, I checked the house one last time. Before rolling out of my driveway, I turned on the radio, attempting to relax for the 45-minute ride to Jacksonville International Airport. There was little to no traffic and I was able to arrive in record time. After parking the car in the long term parking lot, I proceeded to check in at the kiosk, and began walking down to the designated boarding area. Thank goodness I didn't have a long wait. Once I boarded the plane, I nestled in my seat. As we rolled down the runway, I stared out the window; next thing I knew, I was awakened by the overhead announcement.

"Ladies and gentlemen, we are descending and will be landing at JFK in twenty minutes."

Pulling the notepad out of my purse, I reviewed my notes. I sighed as I realized there was nothing I could do until I got there. So, I decided to wait to assess the situation in person.

It has always been a challenge for me when I go to pick up a rental at JFK airport, but this time it was a piece of cake and I was so grateful.

Dad knew I was coming soon but didn't know the exact date or time. Three hours earlier, I was in my car headed to the airport, now I was back on the road in a rental leaving one. All the anxious thoughts dissipated, and I became excited about surprising him. Rearview and side mirrors checked, buckled up, GPS on, radio search fell upon a gospel station. With my foot on the gas, I was ready to take the quickest route through New York City to New Haven, Connecticut.

As I saw my exit up ahead, concerning thoughts began squirreling through my mind again. Before leaving Florida, I had looked online to see what kind of facility Dad was temporarily residing in but remembered that most often pictures on the internet can be deceiving.

I took a deep breath as I thought, "I'm about to find out what is going on." I exhaled as I cautiously pulled in the parking lot, trying to assess the place. It seemed promising that it was a rehabilitation center, so I assumed that Dad's stay here would only be for a short period of time. From the outside, the center didn't look too bad, but I decided to reserve judgment until I was able to see the interior.

There was a lot of construction going on, detour signs were posted on every wall. As soon as I was indoors, I signed in at the desk and the security guard gave me a pass that denoted the floor where Dad was residing. I opened my mouth to say something, but before I could ask, he pointed in the direction of the elevator. Before the doors closed, I pushed the number for the floor, and it seemed like it took forever. Instead of one floor at a time, it felt like the elevator was climbing one step at a time. Ding, the doors opened.

I hear a faint sound from a television. I looked up. In front of me was nothing but a concrete wall. It was so quiet that I could hear myself breathing. I took a deep breath and deliberately poked my head out. I swung my head to the left, then right, then left again, tiptoeing forward. I noticed that the hallway up ahead branched out into the shape of a "Y". I had no clue which way to go, so I walked from one end of the corridor to another, but none of them led me to Dad.

I turned around and went down the other hallway. This was just as confusing. There were several doors to try. I felt like I was on an episode of *Let's Make A Deal*. I had three choices: the left, the right, or the middle door. As I pulled open the middle door and somehow set off the alarm, I gasped for air!

My feet were immovable, stuck to the floor. I thought any second now a security guard, a nurse, or someone would come running my way, but no one did. No one came to see who had entered or left this corridor. After a few seconds, I became suspicious.

"What kind of place is this?" I muttered to myself. Why are there alarms on the doors if no one pays any attention to them? In spite of the glaring sound, I carefully kept walking through the passageway.

Up ahead was a nurse's station, but for some reason, I decided to go the other direction. Still proceeding in a quiet manner around the corner, I ended up in another hallway. Tears began to collect in my eyes, I felt lost, and I could only imagine how Dad must have felt being here all alone.

I walked a few more steps before I heard someone call my name, "Sheri." No one knew I was here, and I'm sure they didn't know my name. So, I thought I was hearing things. I tried to hide my face and quickly wiped the tears away. Slowly turning to my left, my glasses were fogged up from crying, so all I saw was the shadow of a man. With hesitation I walked toward him, still not sure who it was. As I got closer, no one could be mistaken for him. My heart was leaping but I didn't want to cause a commotion. I moved my feet to a faster pace. Faster. Faster.

"Dad," I whispered with each step, "Dad!" Once I caught up to him, we hugged each other and I said aloud, "Dad."

Extreme Makeover

I was able to sign Dad out of the rehabilitation center and for the next three weeks, we were together just about every day. Every evening before we departed, we planned the following day's adventures. I say adventure, because even though we started out each day with a cup of coffee, no day was the same. From greeting everyone in our favorite place (Dunkin Donuts), to walking into a store to get our favorite chocolate candy bar (Hershey's).

I was so grateful to the Lord for how things were working out. Dad was in a much better state than I had anticipated. Though I did not care for the place he was in, every time I felt sorry for him, Dad's words echoed in my mind, "Sheri, don't you worry about anything, God's Got It."

Even though during his stay in the rehabilitation facility Dad was getting stronger and stronger, the case manager communicated that she wasn't too sure of when he would be released or if he would be able to return to living on his own. This news I didn't dare share with Dad, at least not yet. I made an appointment with the care counselor. My thought was to work on a care plan together. Two possibilities to entertain: extend the hours of an aide, thus enabling him to return to his apartment or locating an assisted living facility that he would agree upon. All along, being realistic, I prayed that whichever way it transpired that God would give my dad the mindset to accept it.

Over our morning coffee, out of nowhere, Dad brought up the subject, "Hey, let's start looking for a place, just in case I can't go back home." I was shocked. I had just prayed the night before and God was answering my prayer quickly. I contacted the care counselor and asked for a list of vacancies in facilities that were on a bus line as Dad wanted to remain as mobile as possible.

I let my sister in on the plan and we mapped out our day. Naturally, all three of us had to start the day at Dad's favorite place. While we sipped on a cup of coffee, we rehearsed and reminded each other of our plan. Once we were all in agreement, off we went. We drove from one place to another, and at each place, my sister and I tried to hide our dissatisfaction from Dad. Once we were back in the car, Dad would voice whether the place had met his approval. The ultimate choice was his, but we all agreed that we wouldn't let Dad accept anything less than the lifestyle he had lived before this recent incident.

We ate lunch, finished out our day, and dropped Dad back at the rehab center. That night, before I closed my eyes, I wrote a prayer in my journal.

"Lord, it breaks my heart. Today Dad felt like You have forsaken him. I pray that Dad understands and holds onto his faith and in the truth that You have his best interest at heart. Help him to say once again, 'Don't Worry About Anything. God's Got It'."

Our hunting for the right place was like the tale of the *Three Little Bears*. This one is too small, this one is too expensive, and all of a sudden, this one was just right. We finally found one that Dad liked. But of course, there was a hiccup, it had an eight-month waiting list. We had to decide what to do in the meantime.

The next day we discussed with the care counselor if we could proceed with working on plans that would allow Dad to remain in his apartment until a vacancy came up for the assisted living facility. It took a few days to get approval from various agencies, but she agreed. Dad was provided care for 12 hours, and at night, he would be able to manage alone. We came to a mutual consensus that being able to sleep in his own bed would help with his recovery. But little did I know that Dad had planned this all along. Dad said he was going to prove to them that he was able to live in his own apartment.

Since Dad hadn't been in his apartment for a few months, we needed to go and tidy it up. While we waited for a release date, my siblings and I went to see what we were up against. As we entered his building, we bumped into the office manager (Ms. Sheila). She and the Extreme Makeover Guru (Mr. George), let us know that Dad had been on the waiting list for some upgrades to his apartment and they would have them completed before he returned home. I couldn't think of anything better. Dad's apartment was about to receive an extreme makeover. While they worked on the inside, I went shopping. Dad needed new household items to go with his upgrades.

We tried to explain to Dad what was going on. He's funny. Dad didn't see anything wrong with his apartment the way it was. More than likely because it meant Dad would have to stay a few days extra at the rehab facility. When release day finally came, and we walked into his place, Dad couldn't believe what he saw. Tears rolled from his eyes down his cheeks. I wasn't sure if Dad was just glad to be home or that he was glad to be in his *new* home. His place had brand new wood floors, new light fixtures, freshly painted, new towels, shower curtain, bed, bedspread . . . the whole kit and caboodle.

Dad was so elated until he looked in his cabinets and fridge. He turned around and said, "What did you all do with my food?"

I explained to Dad that a lot of his food had expired and that we were going to go shopping and replace everything with fresh groceries. Dad nodded. He was too excited to let anything mess up this day.

Dad walked around his place, and he said it was fit for a king. Dad was grateful for the new beginning. As he turned around and looked at me, he smiled, and I knew what was next.

"Sheri, I didn't worry about anything, God's Got It!"

His Journals

Even the simplest of things can be passed down from one generation to another. Some years earlier I received a few 1-subject notebooks, Dad's journals. Thinking that his journaling was just something he did to pass the time, I realized that it was more than a passing thing for him. After cleaning out his apartment and finding years of notebooks, turns out these were his thoughts etched in his journals. As I read them, from one page to one journal at a time, I was blessed to have them in my possession. I felt the tears falling from my eyes, and at the same time, a sense of comfort overcame me. Throughout the days, months, and years, you can see his petitions, and a few pages later, were the answers to those very prayers.

March 11, 2000, I sent my father a copy of my first published manuscript. Dad called and said he enjoyed it and asked how it came about.

"I was going through a dark period in my life and felt like I had no one to talk to, so I would journal my thoughts. Most evenings, I would call my mom and share entries with her."

After several months of listening to me, Mom urged me to go to the doctor. Several tests later, the doctor said I was smack dab in the midst of menopause. What I was going through were some of the symptoms of this common season of life.

My mom continued to listen to my stories. About a year later, Mom encouraged me to write a book. Actually, she made me promise. Mom shared her story of how she went through menopause with little to no understanding of what was going on with her body. She told me she felt all alone, misunderstood, and because of the type of treatment or lack of it back in her day, Mom suffered in silence. Mom said that just listening to what I was experiencing was enough for her to make me promise to write a book, that other women needed to hear my story, they needed to know they were not alone.

I told Dad how I had giggled at the thought. I knew nothing about writing a book. I continued to journal, but my show-and-tell hour ceased as Mom's health began to decline. While I knew Mom had a way with words (she helped me with my essays when I was in school), it wasn't till my mom's passing, as I was clearing out her belongings that I found her journals. During my phone call with Dad, we both agreed journaling was a family affair.

By the end of our conversation, the topic took a different turn. Dad asked me if I had something to write with, I said yes. Dad began to dictate his requests: Dad wanted to be cremated and for me to donate his books and his clothes.

I began to get nervous. I didn't like the sound of this. I had a recollection of a few weeks before she passed, I had a conversation like this with Mom. Once we made all the arrangements, soon after, Mom departed the land of the living.

Death, especially the death of a loved one, has a way of waking up a desire deep inside of one to really live. Everyday we are alive is a reason to share our experiences with others, in hopes that they can be encouraged and empowered to live not only beyond our journal entries but live passionately because of them.

Our relationship wasn't that of a typical father and daughter. It took us years to stop trying to change each other and really get to know and accept one another. Then there was a reversal in roles, from me relying on him as an adult, to him relying on me as his confidant and caregiver.

I mention in my mom's book, *Woman of Excellence: The Ministry of My Mother,* how she hungered and thirsted for her earthly father. The lack of a relationship with her dad left her wanting. But what she was looking for her dad wasn't able or (it appears) he wasn't willing to give her. It was only when Mom came to know her heavenly Father that she was transformed. Mom found that all her needs were supplied, and her wants were met in ways that she had never experienced. She found that the love of God superseded the love of any human being.

I was now seeing Dad going through a similar experience in his relationship with the Lord. Dad knew that no matter what he went through, God's Got It. Yes, Dad still pressed through times of disappointment and discouragement, but none of that could change his mind.

And so, the apple doesn't fall far from the tree. Growing up in a single parent home, I dreamed of what it would be like if my dad lived in the same household. Society has set us up for failure. Television shows depict what a healthy family should look like when all the while we lose sight that it is just art and entertainment, and most of the time, it's not imitating life. The small screen emulates a way of life that for the majority of us is unattainable, but somehow, we continue to believe the hype.

My Side of The Story

As a young girl, Dad came over several times a month and took me on short day trips. We'd often visit my aunts (one of his sisters' homes) or an unexpected stop at Dunkin Donuts. I'd order hot chocolate and a glazed donut, and he would have a cup of coffee. As I scarfed down my donut and sipped my piping hot beverage, we'd talk. Those are times that I hope to never forget. Each trip, I was fed spiritually as well as naturally. These father and daughter times bonded us together, and for a period of time, erased all feelings of abandonment.

As a teenager, I began to resent the length of time that grew between our visits. Dad wouldn't call, or when he did, Dad would make promises he didn't keep. I became angry, which led to rebellion. I now see that I acted out in an attempt to get Dad's attention. I couldn't understand what could be more important to him than our times together.

As I grew up, we tried to stay in touch and maintain some type of closeness, but life got in the way and we grew apart. Years went by, and I had my own children. During a school project, one of them had to make a family tree. It was then I realized that they didn't know my dad, their grandfather. One day I got tired of making up stories about Dad, so after they went to bed, I wrote him a letter. The letter spewed out how I felt but ended with the statement that all I wanted was for Dad to have a relationship with us (me and my children . . . his grandchildren).

When I relocated to Connecticut, a few years after I wrote the letter, Dad was one of the first people to visit me. We reconnected and promised to do better about staying in touch with one another.

Dad and I embraced, and it was like we never skipped a beat. We didn't have to go to our favorite spot. We had a cup of instant coffee, sat at the kitchen table, and made up for lost time. That night, I got my answers to the school project.

Some thought we had a perfect father and daughter relationship. People only saw the outside; they had no idea how it took years to put the pieces of our relationship back together. We were both determined to love one another unconditionally, that is what made the difference. Ask me how long it took, I don't honestly remember. All I know is the more I came to know and accept the love of God, my heavenly Father, I in turn viewed Dad the way God saw him and my love for my earthly father was rekindled. I loved Dad simply for who he was, my dad. I loved Dad for the things that he did, and I made a conscious decision to not dwell on what he didn't do.

It is vital that family members communicate and share the history and heritage of one generation to another. Knowledge is power, it has the ability to dictate how we perceive and understand one another. Once I obtained information about my dad's family history and how he was raised, etc., I came to know that a large portion of his disappearing from my life was due to Dad's mental illness.

Dad had been misdiagnosed for years and was unable to help himself or give me what I thought I needed. This is where God steps in, in those times when we look for people, especially family members to give us what they may not be capable of giving. God in His infinite love, mercy, and grace, if we let Him, is waiting to fill our cups.

Our restoration, the revival of our relationship as father and daughter came through that school project. We became intentional and deliberate about staying connected. In addition, how Dad emotionally and mentally supported me, and stayed with me during Mom's illness changed how I saw him, and that changed our story.

1993

Listening to Christian radio has become one of Dad's regular activities. But lately, Dad noticed that he didn't see a great reaching out to those who needed it the most. Dad wrote that pastors have their own flock, and they seem to be satisfied preaching to their own congregation. What about the people on the streets – the homeless, the drug addicts, the mentally ill, and the widows. The statistics seem to be multiplying and there doesn't seem to be anyone who cares for them.

This entry ended with him praying for the laborers because the harvest is plentiful, but the laborers were few (*Matthew 9:37 NIV*).

1994

March 6th

Dad wasn't feeling too good these days. He didn't know what to do, Dad just felt confused. In his journals, Dad wrote a prayer asking God for His help. He felt like he was frozen in time, standing still in one place, not going anywhere. Dad wrote that in spite of everything, he counted his blessings. All of a sudden, his entry made a shift, from him to others. Dad wrote, "What I want to pray for are mostly for other people: my mother and my children for all their needs to be met."

June 7th

Today Dad's journal entry was a praise to God. Dad thanked God in advance as he looked forward to something special happening today.

October 1st

Today is one of those days where Dad felt hopeless, roaming around without a purpose. Another journal entry that turned into a prayer.

"Lord, don't pay my groaning any attention. I'm not hungry. I have a roof over my head and clothes on my back. I have everything I need."

"When I feel like I am all alone, You change my perspective. Once again, I am having to be reminded of how blessed I am. Today I will go and visit family, especially those that cannot get out."

Later that day was an additional entry. Dad wrote that he is noticing a pattern in his journal. He prays and cries out, and God answers. "Thank you, Lord – again."

October 18th

Today Dad's prayer is for his mother, Dad was so thankful to have her in his life. This week, she is turning ninety-two years old. Dad acknowledges in his entry that he didn't have a father, but that God blessed him with a mother who is incredibly special in his life.

I concur with what my dad said about Grandma Simmons (that's what I called her). She was a very special lady. She had extraordinary qualities, which reminded me of the Proverbs 31 woman depicted in the Bible. Grandma Simmons was a woman of noble character. She was worth far more than rubies. Though a widow before I was born, I believe her husband had full confidence in her. She didn't bring harm, but good all the days of her life. Grandma Simmons sewed and worked with her hands. She grew what she could and shopped for what she couldn't grow.

Grandma Simmons could make something out of nothing, whenever and however she could, she'd find a way to save some money. She was "old school." Here are some things my family shared, that I forgot about her. She only used a comb in her hair and washed it in rainwater. She washed all of her lingerie by hand. She wasn't one to eat huge plates of food. She ate lots of bananas, liked Wonder Bread and Welch's grape jelly. She would make her own milk. Speaking of milk, that concoction was an acquired taste. I believe it was a mixture of powdered Carnation milk and some other ingredient. At her table, you dared not tell her you didn't like it, you simply gulped it down with a quickness.

I have so many memories of my times at her house. One that I have an appreciation for today, is that when the news came on, Grandma Simmons took the phone off the cradle and you sat by her and didn't move until the news went off.

Most of the time, the weekends were filled with fun. If she wasn't teaching me how to sew, we were out in the garden in her backyard. I learned everything from pulling weeds, picking tomatoes and collard greens, to cleaning and snapping green beans. Once we were done, while she finished up in the kitchen, I had the task of licking and placing S & H Green Stamps in their corresponding catalogs.

S&H Green Stamps was a line of trading stamps popular in the United States from the 1930s until the late 1980s. They were distributed as part of a rewards program operated by the Sperry & Hutchinson company (S&H), founded in 1896 by Thomas Sperry and Shelley Byron Hutchinson. During the 1960s, the company promoted its rewards catalog as being the largest publication in the United States.

I remember the excitement I felt when Grandma Simmons would receive stamps at the checkout counter of supermarkets. Back at her house, after the books were filled, we'd count them and look in the catalog to see what we could redeem.

Grandma Simmons had compassion for the poor and the needy, a characteristic that our family inherited. We all called her "blessed" and praised her for she was a woman who did noble things. She was beautiful, yet not conceited. Grandma Simmons was a woman who feared the Lord and we are so blessed to have lived alongside her. Still today, there are countless generations of Simmons' gleaning from the life she lived before us.

October 27th

Like his mom, Dad loved to watch the news and keep up with current events. His journal started off, "It's a clear night with limitless possibilities. There has been a milestone within the past couple of days with the signing of the peace treaty between Israel and Jordan."

Main Points of Israel-Jordan Peace Treaty

On 10/26/94, Prime Minister Yitzhak Rabin and Prime Minister Abdul-Salam Majali signed the Treaty of Peace between the State of Israel and the Hashemite Kingdom of Jordan, the second peace treaty Israel has signed since its independence.

The peace treaty with Jordan comprises 30 articles, five annexes which address boundary demarcations, water issues, police cooperation, environmental issues, and mutual border crossings, and six maps.

The main provisions of the treaty are as follows:

1. International boundary: The Agreement delimits the agreed international boundary between Israel and Jordan including territorial waters and airspace.

    These rights will remain in force for 25 years and will be renewed automatically for the same period unless either country wishes to terminate the arrangement, in which case, consultations will be taken.

2. Security: The two parties will refrain from any acts of belligerency or hostility, will ensure that no threats of violence against the other party originate from within their territory, and undertake to take necessary and effective measures to prevent acts of terrorism.

3. Water: Israel and Jordan have agreed on allocations of water from the Jordan and Yarmouk Rivers and from Araba/Arava groundwaters.

4. Freedom of Passage: Nationals from both countries and their vehicles will be permitted freedom of movement through open roads and border-crossings.

5. Places of Historical and Religious Significance: There will be freedom of access to the places of religious and historical significance.

6. Refugees and Displaced Persons: The parties recognize the human problems caused by the conflict in the Middle East, and agree to alleviate them on a bilateral level and to try to resolve them through three channels:
    - The quadripartite committee with Egypt and the Palestinians with regard to displaced persons.
    - The Multilateral Working Group on Refugees.
    - Negotiations in a framework to be agreed upon – bilateral

or otherwise in conjunction with permanent status negotiations detailed in the Declaration of Principles.

7. Normalization of Relations between Israel and Jordan: The peace treaty deals not only with an end to war, but also normalization. Jordan and Israel will maintain good neighborly relations by cooperating in many spheres on joint projects. Among the projects are development of energy and water sources, protecting the natural environment, joint tourism development, and the development of the Jordan Rift Valley.

Dad ended the entry stating, we have to start somewhere, and this is as good a place as any. One little accomplishment could mushroom (no pun intended) into something beyond our imagination.

October 30th

Dad went down to the New Haven Green and had lunch. Before Dad went home, he sat on a bench and fed the pigeons what he had left.

I remember when I was a little girl this was also one of our favorite pastimes. The first time I experienced it, I thought it was a joke. Dad picked me up for our Saturday outing. Dad said, he had a change of plans. I tried not to let it show, but I was a little ticked off. I was looking forward to having donuts and hot chocolate at our favorite place. Anyway, it didn't seem like my attitude was going to change Dad's mind, so I sat back and decided to enjoy the ride.

My curiosity started to peak as I realized we were headed downtown. Dad parked the car, and he nodded in the direction of the car door. I took it that it was for me to get out. We started walking toward the mall. The closer we got, the stronger the aroma. This scent was different from that of Jiffy Popcorn. Karmel Korn was said to be the best popcorn in all the world, well at least in Chapel Square Mall in New Haven, Connecticut. As Dad ordered a large, I knew dinner was about to be spoiled because my mind was made up to enjoy every kernel.

I tried to multi-task: walk and eat at the same time. He suggested we go sit on the Green. Dad said, "Hold on tight." We weren't going to get another bag if I dropped it. I wasn't too worried about that. In my mind, it tasted so good, my thought was I'd probably be done before we even reached the bench.

My bag was half full, or in Dad's assessment, half empty. Before I could nuzzle my bottom on the bench, here they came, gathering all around us. I clenched my bag and looked at Dad, "I'm not gonna have to share, right?"

Dad said, "Feed them."

Not sure if I said it aloud, but I was not about to give these pigeons my popcorn. Dad repeated himself and grabbed a handful of my popcorn and threw it out in front of us.

Holding in my urge to scream, it looked like we were in the middle of an Alfred Hitchcock movie. It was like we rang the dinner bell. The grass disappeared and there were seagulls, pigeons, and black crows before us. When all the popcorn was gone, I lifted up my feet and scurried across the Green making our way back to the car. With each step we took, I turned and looked behind me; they were following us. Though it was a waste of perfectly good popcorn to me, I grabbed Dad's hand to feel secure and said, "Thank you, that was kind of fun."

This spontaneous adventure turned out to be a regular one for us, especially when the weather was nice. Dunkin in the winter and The Green in the summer. It may sound ordinary to some, but these are the kind of memories that are etched on my heart.

December 23rd

Dad hoped that this Christmas would be a happy holiday. He was aware that many won't get what they want, but Dad prayed that they would at least get what they needed.

1995

January 11th

Even though Dad knew his current situation, he still yearned to be gainfully employed. Dad would often get the newspaper just to see what kind of jobs were out there. He circled some and even made a few phone calls. But after speaking with one or two employers, Dad joked around about contacting them one day when he was ready to go back to work. After he hung up, Dad reassured himself that he was in a good place.

January 20th

Dad woke up with a heart full of thanksgiving. He was thankful for his family, those near and far. Dad mentioned how he adored his mother and wished he were in a place to take care of her. But he knew that she was satisfied with him being stable and able to care for himself.

March 2nd

As Dad took the bus downtown, he noticed an increase in unemployment, homelessness, drugs, alcoholism, and prostitution. He journaled how this wasn't an issue for one person, but all hands would have to be on deck. Dad resolved himself to do what he could do. With his tender heart, Dad shared what he did have with those who were without and left the politicking to the politicians.

March 3rd

Dad went to church today and journaled how he enjoyed the service very much. He was raised in church and had a great appreciation when the choir sang, and the pastor brought "a word" that resonated in his spirit.

He prayed for one of his friends who was struggling with a problem. Dad didn't care to know how it started, he only wanted him to find a remedy for the sake of his family.

Dad wrote how he was so grateful; he knew he was a living miracle. After all he had been through, Dad knew his luck ran out, but his blessings kept flowing. He thanked God for hearing his cry and answering his prayers.

April 21st

The Oklahoma City bombing was in the news. Dad couldn't make sense of this, so he wrote a prayer for all involved, the victims, their families, and friends.

The Oklahoma City bombing occurred when a truck packed with explosives was detonated on April 19, 1995, outside the Alfred P. Murrah Federal Building in Oklahoma City, Oklahoma, killing 168 people and leaving hundreds more injured. The blast was set off by anti-government militant Timothy McVeigh, who in 2001 was executed for his crimes. His co-conspirator Terry Nichols was sentenced to life in prison.

April 24th

Dad woke up perplexed about the society we live in. He saw the struggle of mankind and wished that things could be different. Dad wanted to do something, so he prayed, while getting dressed to go down to his favorite coffee shop.

Everywhere Dad went, his arrival reminded you of the character Norm on the sitcom, *Cheers*. Everyone would turn around and say, "Hey, Reg." He looked around and observed the establishment. Dad was checking to be sure that everyone had something to eat or drink. If you didn't, he'd walk over to you and ask what you were drinking.

Often when I was visiting Dad and we'd go out, I would be a tad concerned that someone would take advantage of him. Dad never blinked an eye about his personal safety. He believed that if you treat people right, they will treat you with respect. Our fears never came true, actually the opposite happened. When Dad had this last accident, he fell in his favorite place. From the owner to the employees, he was cared for. Our family is forever grateful to them. They took care of Dad like he was a member of their family.

May 7th

Dad didn't take the small things for granted. Today before he could ask the gentleman in front of the coffee shop how he was, the man beat Dad to it. Dad was taken back. Normally he was the one doing the asking. He was always checking to see how others were doing. Today, Dad was on the receiving end and he journaled that it felt good.

June 12th

This journal entry was special to me. I read how Dad drafted several letters to people in his city (local officials) to see what kind of assistance was out there for the poor and neglected on the streets (those who are unemployed and in need of medical treatment).

From the looks of the letter it was in rough draft form, but that doesn't mean that he never finalized, mailed, or even received a response.

I could feel my lips slowly rising, forming a smile on my face. I thought in amazement about how much you can learn about a person from their life, even after they have passed. I found comfort in knowing that our family has a long lineage of caring and compassion for others. This innate gift was probably nothing new to Dad; he seemed to know it and accepted that we were born to be a blessing.

In 2014, our family had planned a family gathering. We are blessed with our very own genealogists (Melvin & Cleo Graham). They worked tirelessly traveling and researching and verifying our history – providing us with volumes of information, images, and documents.

While the amount of information they were able to uncover would appear to be conclusive, they have found that there is still more to be revealed. They traced our ancestors all the way back to 1793. As they recited the names, dates, and places of birth, it made it seem as if our ancestors were in our midst.

From the presentation, we were briefed that we are from a lineage of givers. Our family history was full of servants from pastors, elders, deacons, deaconesses to government officials. Their research also uncovered that our ancestors were slaves. Brought to America from

Africa, broken but proud people, who worked their fingers to the bone while educating themselves. They worked together to eventually own a piece of land where they built a church, Simmons Ridge Baptist Church in Edgefield, South Carolina.

I'd like to think one of our family mottos is a saying that Dad shared one day. "Jesus reached down to him, so that he could reach out to others." All Dad wanted to do, like our descendants, was to be of service, to be an asset to the community. I saw that after the discovery of our family lineage, Dad was comforted, knowing that his hunger to help the least of these was indeed an inborn character trait.

If you ever spent a day with my dad, you would see that there is a good possibility that his ministry did indeed come to fruition. Maybe not in the way you or I would have it, but nevertheless Dad wasn't one to tell you what he was going to do, he just did it.

I remember one day when we were on our Dunkin Donuts run, Dad leaned over to see the gas needle. He suggested that we not wait till it was near empty. I agreed and made my way to a brand name gas station. Abruptly Dad said, "No, go over there, pull in this gas station" waving his arm and pointing his finger at the same time he spoke.

From the tone of Dad's voice, mine was not to ask why, it was to do what he said. As we pulled up into the gas aisle, I wondered why he chose this one. But instead of trying to dissect Dad's command, I obeyed, knowing that he had a reason. Dad turned to me and said, "I'll pay for the gas."

Dad hopped out of the car and I put it in park. My eyes followed his every step. On the stoop at the entrance to the gas station sat a middle-aged lady, who didn't look any older than fifty. She looked like she had been sitting there for a while. I started to feel sorry for her. I looked closer and she had her chin resting on her chest, with a sunken look on her face.

She must have heard footsteps because I don't remember hearing him call her name. She looked upwards and when she saw Dad, her eyes lit up and a smile made its way to her face. Though I couldn't hear, it was evident that they exchanged a few sentences. The car was already turned off and in order to crack the window to hear what they were saying, I'd have to turn the car back on. I dared not, that would probably make them suspicious. So, I just sat there looking, while trying to read lips.

Dad reached in his pocket. His hand came out with what looked like a few dollars. Dad waved to her and walked inside to pay for the gas. He returned to the car and proceeded around to the driver's side, grabbed the nozzle, and continued pumping gas until the tank was filled.

He settled the fuel dispenser in the cradle and got back inside the car. I waited patiently and tried to gauge the right moment to ask him a question. "Dad, why did you give that lady money?"

Dad turned to look at me, and he had a combined look of compassion and sorrow on his face. His voice was low, "I'd rather give her the money than see her on the corner selling herself."

I fought back the tears. I wanted to go and hug her and take her somewhere safe. But Dad said, "This is what she does day after day. So, until she does otherwise, this is one way I can help try to keep her off the streets."

At first, I was about to judge why he would enable her, but after talking about it further, I realized that we cannot make people change. They have to want it for themselves. But we can love them through their mess, which is what often gets the wheels of change in motion.

These encounters were an everyday experience for him. When you think of Dad's life, the good he tried to do on the streets of New Haven, it may seem odd to some, but just ask anyone in the New Haven area about his character.

Actually, I didn't have to ask, they told me. When Dad went from the hospital to rehab for those months and returned back visiting his favorite spot, people on the street, in Dunkin, and in his neighborhood missed him. The day he got out, wherever we went, they had no problem showing how much they missed and loved him.

One day at a red light, a guy came over to the car yelling, "Uncle Reggie, Uncle Reggie, where have you been? We were worried about you. No one knew where you were."

I looked at the guy trying to recognize him.

I said, "Dad, how is he related to us?"

Dad said, "He's not. He just calls me his uncle."

The guy came over to the car and shared how he felt about Dad. That was one of those moments I still to this day wished I had recorded with my phone.

"Superman" is what the guy called him. Was this what enabled him to see beyond what others saw or thought of themselves? Dad saw them as a human being, someone who had a purpose or needed help finding it. This is the very ingredient that we all need to make this world a better place.

August 12th

How fitting is today's journal entry. Mark 8:36, What good is it for someone to gain the whole world yet forfeit their soul?

Material things are a necessity to survive, but materialism can cause destruction. Most have more than enough to share with someone else. The problem is whether we choose to or not.

Another entry that is turned into a prayer. He prayed for people to open their heart and try to be a blessing to one another.

September 14th

Lately it appears the conversations of the day have shifted. People are less tolerant with one another and expect people to see it their way or the highway.

Wasn't it Rodney King that said, "Can't we all just get along?" Dad realized that not everyone saw things the way he did, so he resolved to not discount anyone just because of their beliefs. Dad saw these encounters as opportunities to learn about one another and from one another.

October 29th

Dad had a heart attack and felt like time was running out for him. He asked God for help, to help him get better.

November 16th

Dad prayed that God would take care of his family. He hoped that he did some good, that he was able to make a difference in someone's life while he was in the land of the living.

November 25th

Dad woke up today with not one complaint, he looked around and saw that every need he had was provided for him. He was grateful for the things he had, a quiet and simple life, one filled with joy, hope, and love.

December 31st

It's New Year's Eve, and from the entry, Dad appeared to be feeling better. Dad wrote that this upcoming year he was going to make a deliberate effort and make the necessary changes in his life.

1996

January 28th

Dad wrote how he remembered when he first became ill working for the Navy Department in Washington D.C. at the Pentagon. Lots of medication, lots of hospitalizations, what's next?

1997

January 14th

Dad had written over and over how the only reason he was who he was, and was where he was, was because of his love and faith in God. Today's entry, Why do I read the Bible?
1) It gives substance to my faith.
2) It stabilizes me in times of trouble.
3) It enables me to handle the Bible correctly.
4) It equips me to detect and confront error, and
5) It makes me confident in my walk with the Lord.

April 25th

Dad woke up this morning thanking God for His goodness. Today life didn't seem so dim. There were times in the past, where Dad wanted to die. But today he felt like it was a day worth living.

November 10th

Today's entry was spent praying for others. Throughout Dad's journals, they tell the story of Dad in times of intercession – praying for others. Often, Dad would ask for a blessing for himself, but most of all, his prayers were for others.

Another trait I inherited, I love praying with and for other people.

December 9th

Dad was praying about his current living situation and he felt like there was a change coming and he wrote that he would be patient while waiting for it.

December 10th

Dad prayed for each of his children, he wrote down our names and each entry was personalized to what he believed we needed. I giggled when I read about our youngest brother. I noticed Dad's prayer for him was the longest.

I think it is a priceless inheritance when a child can read about or know that their parent is praying for them. I hope my siblings know just how much he prayed for us. Dad might not have been able to do some things that we wished or thought he should have done. But I believe Dad's prayers kept us in other ways that I consider to be priceless.

1998

January 25th

Another entry about Ronnie (our youngest brother). Dad wrote that there wasn't much financially he could do to help him, so he resolved to pray for him.

Ronnie passed on May 22, 2016. Typing this with the realization that the dates caught my attention. Strange, and probably no coincidence, Ronnie and Dad died in the same month. Four years and nine days apart from one another (sad face).

September 12th

Dad prayed for Mr. Brown, he had lost his wife and needed a financial blessing. Dad wrote that though he hasn't lost a wife, but he did lose his brother, and to lose a wife had to be extremely hard for his friend.

October 27th

Dad wrote an entry of thanksgiving for his brother-in-law (James Ingram), he loved him and was thankful how he provided for his sister and their children.

1999

February 18th

Dad reminisces how in 1966 in Washington, D.C., he got on his knees for the first time. There has never been a time since then that he doubted his faith in Jesus Christ. My dad continued to write that his journal entries were a way he could be sure his family and friends knew his thoughts, desires, and prayers after he was gone, especially how much my dad loved God.

February 19th

Dad writes how his life is good and he is in the waiting stage of going home with the Lord. He feels that he has done and accomplished everything that he had to do on this earth . . . so Dad is just going to watch, wait, and see.

2000

January 30th

Dad writes how he wanted to start the new year out right. Though he could complain, Dad looked around and reminded himself that he didn't lack any good thing. There are several areas of Dad's life that he would like to be another way, but he is learning to focus on what he has and less on what he doesn't.

November 15th

Dad writes though the system has labeled him as disabled in his mind, Jesus has enabled him in the spirit.

2003

January 12th

Dad's mom (Grandma Simmons) passed away. She was the best thing that ever happened to him.

2009

April 15th

Dad's prayer today was one of thanksgiving. As far as I can see, God has cleaned him up very well. Dad sat in his home, wondering what to say, all he could think of was, "THANK YOU."

The previous year was a tough one, Dad was placed in a temporary residence and our mom died in November.

But in the midst of it all, Dad would remind me, "God's Got It" and we needed to see the light at the end of the tunnel. And the light indeed did come on. Dad received the best Christmas present one could get. He was about to move into his own apartment. Everything in his apartment was brand new . . . except for him. Well actually maybe he was, Dad had a new perspective on life.

He was grateful for his new residence, but he made mention of a bonus blessing. Dad was within walking distance to you know where . . . yep, his favorite place.

2010

February 15th

Dad writes how today he was sitting on the bench outside of his apartment. He had a full cup of coffee in his hand and a heart full of thanksgiving. Dad thanked the Lord again for being alive and his health getting better day by day.

2020

I noticed the journaling slowed down significantly, especially around 2010. I wonder if Dad was settled and didn't feel the need to jot down his thoughts any longer.

Monday, June 1st, I was sitting at my workstation at home, in the midst of a Skype meeting. The phone rang. I checked the caller ID, I said hmm, to myself. We would talk often, but not so early in the day. I placed the Skype call on hold.

"Hello," I said.

"Sheri, your dad is gone."

I'm listening and thinking somebody is playing a cruel joke on me. I just talked to Dad Sunday before he lay down to take a nap. In between the tears, the nurse began to share how she and the home health aide arrived and it was out of the norm for Dad not to answer the door. So, they called 911. When the paramedics arrived and they all were able to gain access into his apartment, she described that they found him lying (looking like he was taking a nap) in his bed.

After several attempts to revive my dad, the paramedics were unable to get a pulse. Within the next few moments, they found themselves paralyzed, unable to move their feet. Tears rolled down their faces as a song on the radio came on, and consoled them, that it was alright that he wasn't waking up.

Carry On

This is Dad's last journal entry: *First of all, I would like to thank and praise God for my time here on earth. My health and strength is surprisingly good. At my age, I can look back and see how good God has been to me and my family.*

Some family members have gone on before me. I can honestly say that I'm looking forward to joining them when the time comes. I have plenty to be thankful for, my children and their children.

Life has been hard at times but looking back it is worth it all. I have a great family and at this time I am enjoying every one of them.

I'm told Dad passed sometime between Sunday, May 31 and Monday morning, June 1. After I received that call, in my mind I became an orphan. There was a feeling of emptiness that I still cannot explain. Both of my parents are now gone.

So many thoughts raced through my head, how, what, why. With our nation in the midst of a pandemic (COVID-19), how was I going to get home with the travel restrictions and such, even gatherings, including funerals were being planned in an entirely different manner.

I remember the last conversation that I had with Dad's primary care doctor. We started out with a cordial conversation and before we hung up, he said, "You know your father didn't take his illnesses seriously."

I replied with confidence, "Actually, doctor, my dad didn't let his illnesses stop him from living, what they did, was helped him live every day on purpose."

Yes, Dad you were right, you didn't wake up that morning, and it is all right because "God's Got It" and He has you!

Thank You

43

I'd like to thank the building and property manager, and the superintendent at Dad's apartment building. Each of you went out of your way to ensure Dad's home was fit for a king.

Thank you to our family, your generosity and donations have assisted me in bringing Dad's journals to print. It is our hope that this book will help encourage our readers to remember that tomorrow isn't promised to anyone. That they would live in a way that creates precious memories that will last a lifetime – perhaps some memories will be with a cup of coffee.

Summit

I titled this chapter "Summit" because Dad arrived at the top. In the latter part of his life, Dad reached the peak, the crest, if you will, of his life. He may have started out at the base camp, but Dad ended at the pinnacle.

Dad was given so many labels in lieu of calling him by his name. His name is Reginald Lionel Simmons, and he didn't allow what was written in his medical records to define him.

Growing up over the years, I've heard the whispers, but no one really talked about it in its entirety. As a teen, I used to go visit Dad when he was in the hospital or a care center, but neither the diagnosis nor treatment were discussed. What was said, was that he needed rest, but I never put the pieces together until I began to ask Dad questions myself. To my surprise, he was forthcoming.

"Gee whiz, Sheri, why didn't you ask him earlier?" I said to myself.

I used to find myself wanting to place blame, for all those years that Dad was misdiagnosed. But then I remembered that doctors "practice" medicine, with the end goal (for the most part) to find out what's best for each patient. It is clear that some treatments can be hit or miss, trial and error, until one day they find the right fit. This is one of the reasons why it is vital that family members and those that support the individual who is experiencing any type of mental, emotional, and physical challenge are educated and understand in totality what is going on.

It took years for Dad to find a physician that believed in helping him get better and not just coping. It is unfortunate that for many the medicine and treatment that they are prescribed leave patients feeling worse, instead of better. It is our hope that in sharing Dad's story that at least one person will have hope and see a brighter future.

I am forever grateful that God dispensed the strength and support that enabled Dad to make it through one day at a time. And after several years, Dad's conclusive diagnosis was bipolar disorder.

His journal was filled with additional accounts of his life, but I hope I shared enough to give you a glimpse. His struggles, his hopes, and how in the midst of his darkness, Dad continued to have hope, as he held onto the truth that "God's Got It."

I may sound like a broken record, but education and support are two of a number of things that will make a big difference for those that are experiencing mental illness as well as their family members. It is vital for all involved to come to an understanding that the individual with this challenge is not their disorder. But with a plan (as much as possible) to incorporate coping skills, they may be able to live a meaningful life.

Though most do not like support groups, there are many benefits in surrounding ourselves with those that are making efforts to maintain a productive lifestyle.

According to National Institutes of Mental Health (NNIMH), Bipolar disorder is a chronic or episodic (which means occurring occasionally and at irregular intervals) mental disorder. It can cause unusual, often extreme, and fluctuating changes in mood, energy, activity, and concentration or focus. Bipolar disorder sometimes is called *manic-depressive disorder* or *manic depression*, which are older terms.

Everyone goes through normal ups and downs, but bipolar disorder is different. The range of mood changes can be extreme. In manic episodes, someone might feel very happy, irritable, or "up," and there is a marked increase in activity level. In depressive episodes, someone might feel sad, indifferent, or hopeless, in combination with a very low activity level. Some people have hypomanic episodes, which are like manic episodes, but less severe and troublesome.

Most of the time, bipolar disorder develops or starts during late adolescence (teen years) or early adulthood. Occasionally, bipolar symptoms can appear in children. Although the symptoms come and go, bipolar disorder usually requires lifetime treatment and does not go away on its own. Bipolar disorder can be an important factor in suicide, job loss, and family discord, but proper treatment leads to better outcomes.

This book is not meant to provide any medical terminology or diagnosis for anyone. It is a tool of encouragement. On the Resources page, we have provided information that we hope will shed some light on this disorder. Ultimately, it is vital that you seek medical and professional help and let a doctor assist you with your care. If your loved one is not capable of making decisions regarding their wellbeing, think about becoming their health care advocate. Above all else, don't stop knocking on doors, don't take "no" for an answer. Dad didn't, I didn't, and we hope you won't either.

Resources

For More Information: NIMH website: www.nimh.nih.gov

National Institute of Mental Health
Office of Science Policy, Planning, and Communications
Science Writing, Press, and Dissemination Branch
6001 Executive Boulevard Room 6200, MSC 9663
Bethesda, MD 20892-9663
Phone: 301-443-4513 or
Toll-free: 866-615-NIMH (6464)
TTY: 301-443-8431 or
TTY Toll-free: 866-415-8051
Fax: 301-443-4279
Email: nimhinfo@nih.gov

U.S. Department of Health and Human Services
National Institutes of Health
NIH Publication No. 19-MH-8088

Get Immediate Help in a Crisis: **Call 911** if you or someone you know is in immediate danger or go to the nearest Emergency Room.

National Suicide Prevention Lifeline
Call 1-800-273-TALK (8255); En Español 1-888-628-9454
The Lifeline is a free, confidential crisis hotline that is available to everyone 24 hours a day, seven days a week. The Lifeline connects callers to the nearest crisis center in the Lifeline national network. These centers provide crisis counseling and mental health referrals. People who are

deaf, hard of hearing, or have hearing loss can contact the Lifeline via TTY at 1-800-799-4889.

Crisis Text Line
Text "HELLO" to 741741
The Crisis Text hotline is available 24 hours a day, seven days a week throughout the United States. The Crisis Text Line serves anyone, in any type of crisis, connecting them with a crisis counselor who can provide support and information.

Epilogue

I always like to end my books with an invitation. If you have never asked Jesus to be your Lord and Savior, or if you would like to rededicate your life, PAUSE and consider doing so today. It's as easy as A, B, C.

<u>A</u>dmit
All have sinned and fall short of the glory of God.
—Romans 3:23

<u>B</u>elieve
For God so loved the world that He gave His only begotten Son, that whoever believes in Him should not perish but have everlasting life.
—John 3:16

<u>C</u>all
Whoever calls on the name of the Lord shall be saved.
—Romans 10:13

If you have repeated these A, B, C's, pick a book in the Bible and begin reading.

If you don't have a church home, locate a Bible-believing church, and let them know the decision you have made today! Congratulations and welcome to the family of God.

References

Dedication

Acquaintance vs Friend – https://bit.ly/3qKEsI6
How To Make The Friends You've Always Wanted – https://bit.ly/3foBtmz
What Is The Real Definition Of A True Friend – https://bit.ly/3vppSJM

C-O-F-F-E-E

20+ Good Health Reasons To Drink Coffee – https://bit.ly/3qK7yY7
Healthy Lifestyle Antioxidants – https://mayocl.in/3rL2V1p
Harvesting of Coffee – https://bit.ly/38BTOs1
13 Health Benefits of Coffee, Based on Science – https://bit.ly/3taPNmi
10 Steps from Seed to Cup – https://bit.ly/2Q1tYYd
How Coffee Is Made – https://bit.ly/30IEdCW

1993

Matthew 9:35-38 – https://bit.ly/30IAchz

1994

Mark 14:7 – https://bit.ly/3vkRFLa
S & H Green Stamps – https://bit.ly/3rN4onF
Main Points of Israel-Jordan Peace Treaty – https://bit.ly/2OmkZR2

1995

Mark 8:36 – https://bit.ly/3bHwFGO
Nation & World News – https://bit.ly/3tgxnAD

Summit

Merriam-Webster Dictionary – https://bit.ly/3vkOcwf
Finding the Right Bipolar Disorder Treatment – https://bit.
ly/3eC85Jm

About the Author

Sheri is also the author of *Pausing With God: A Journey Through Menopause* (English & Spanish), *Pausing In His Presence: A Shut-In Experience, A Woman of Excellence: The Ministry of My Mother.* She lives and breathes to simply do God's will. With an inherent desire to "Share the Lord with People", Sheri founded and created the SLP Company. Its goal is to share available resources that can help willing participants be all that God has created them to be.

Sheri is also the founder of *Pausing With God Ministries*, a 501(c)(3) nonprofit organization whose mission is to engage, encourage, and empower women of all ages. Sheri has seen numerous lives transformed. PWGM engages women to turn their weakness into strength and use their gifts and talents to make a difference in their life, their family, and their community.

PWGM encourages women of all ages to understand who they are and empowering them to build authentic relationships and work together to make an impact in our surrounding areas and our world. PWGM equips women to reach their God-given purpose.

Sheri is married and has five adult children, three grandchildren, and a host of sister-friends worldwide. Sheri is a Christian author, counselor, life coach, and mentor. Sheri is available for seminars, conferences, evangelistic outreaches, youth events, Bible studies, workshops, or book signings. To contact Sheri, submit your request by email: PausingWithGod@gmail.com or by U.S. Mail: Pausing With God Ministries P.O. Box 9172 Fleming Island, FL 32006. Or submit your request using this link: https://pausingwithgod.com/contact-us/ on our website (PausingWithGod.com).